A Dwarven Cookbook

Recipes from the Kingdom of Kathaldûm

Stephanie Drummonds
and Daniel Myers

Artwork by Brian Cribb

Copyright © 2011 Stephanie Drummonds & Daniel Myers

2 4 6 8 10 9 7 5 3

ISBN-10: 0615549616
ISBN-13: 978-0615549613

DEDICATION

For my family, who always believe I can. And for my husband John, whose support is without measure – Stephanie.

For Cindy, who is so incredibly tolerant of my odd hobbies, and for Alex and Nico, who are surprisingly willing to try the strange things that their dad cooks – Daniel.

CONTENTS

Introduction

The original text of this cookbook was discovered in an abandoned silver mine. A survey of the site determined that it had once been a major population center, but was seemingly abandoned after the ore veins were played out. The manuscript, approximately one foot square and several inches thick, was beautifully bound in dark green tooled leather, fastened with a brass buckled strap. The text was written in three distinct hands, on well scraped vellum, the pages stained and dog eared from heavy use.

It was found in the ruins of a once vast kitchen on one of the lower, more protected levels of the mine. The kitchen had several open hearths for cooking, as well as ovens chiseled into the surrounding rock. One hearth appears to have been dedicated solely to roasting meats, as the remains of multiple spits were still evident.

The names of the main cooks are not known, making it difficult to determine the exact date of the text. However, one of the menus recorded is noted as being for the Ascension of Thorfil Axewielder as King, which suggests the bulk of the manuscript dates from that period.

Though the text contains three distinct styles of handwriting - two in precise, tightly spaced runes, the third in an unruled runic script - we have decided for the sake of clarity to reproduce all of the source text in a single type face. A blackletter font was chosen over more traditional runes for ease of reading.

While the majority of the recipes from the original text are included, we have chosen not to reproduce the full text. There were an additional seventeen sausage recipes, many of which are duplicates of included recipes or differ only in insignificant ways, as well as more than a dozen recipes for 'specialty meats' (e.g., rat, field mouse, weasel). In these cases, we have chosen the dishes that are most representative of the cuisine, and most accessible to the modern palate.

Additionally, we have grouped like recipes where the original text presented them in an arbitrary order.

Udandizûd (Meats)

The Dwarven word *udandizûd* could be glossed as meaning "animal food", that is to say food made from animals.

From the preponderance of *udandizûd* recipes in the original text, it can be surmised that meats, in great quantity and variety, were the primary staple of the Dwarven diet. Discounting the few pages devoted to potables and sauces, recipes for meat or primarily meat dishes outnumber those for non-meat or *umaralâm* nearly two to one.

One of the most striking details of the text was the extensive variety of meat sources referenced. We have chosen not to include some of the more exotic game recipes, due to difficulty in obtaining the ingredients.

To make Khêndun chicken, roast chickens and chop them well. Then take the meat of a wild boar that has been boiled and chop it and put it with the chickens. Add to this ground rosemary and ginger and pepper and salt, and some wine or vinegar and honey. Put it all into a kettle and boil it, and when it is boiled serve it.

The name of this dish appears to be a reference to a mountain range near Elven lands. This is reflected in the dish, which is one of the few Dwarven recipes to specifically call for chicken. It is likely that this recipe was originally adapted from an Elven one.

Khêndun Chicken

1 lb. chicken, roasted
1 lb. pork, boiled
2 tsp. ground rosemary
1 tsp. ground ginger
1 tsp. salt
½ tsp. pepper
1 cup white wine
1 Tbsp. honey

Chop the chicken and pork well and place in a large pot or skillet. Add remaining ingredients and cook over a medium heat until it comes to a boil. Simmer for about 20 minutes. Serve hot.

Serves 8.

For Gurbok, roast a fowl with fatty bacon until it be done, then chop to small bits. Take andulam and bake in hot fat not too dry. Peel and slice tart apples. In a large pan that is not too deep, layer the andulam, then the apples, then the roast fowl taking care to spice each layer, until the pan be full. Make a condiment of honey, mead and spice and pour thereon. Turn out onto a platter and slice to serve.

According to a recipe in another part of the text, *andulam* are thick slices of day-old bread, which are soaked in milk and eggs, coated in bread crumbs and pan-fried in lard.

Gurbok - Layered Chicken Hot Pot

2 lbs. chicken
¼ lb. bacon
8 slices bread
1 cup milk
2 eggs
bread crumbs
2 Tbsp. lard
½ tsp. coriander
2 tart apples

¼ cup mead
¼ cup honey
¼ tsp. ground coriander

Lay the chicken in a baking dish and cover with the bacon. Roast in a 350°F oven until done. Remove from the oven and chop small.

While the chicken is baking, prepare the andulam. Combine the milk and eggs, dip the slices of bread in this mixture and pan fry until the egg is cooked and the bread is a light golden brown. Remove to a platter and keep warm. Peel and core the apples. Cut into thick slices and fry in the same pan as the *andulam* until they are softened, but not caramelized.

In a lightly greased baking pan, place four slices of the andulam, then a layer of the apples, then a layer of the chopped chicken. Repeat layers of apples and chicken until you have used it all, then finish with the other four slices of andulam. Combine the honey, mead and coriander, and pour it over the layers. Let the *Gurbok* sit for a short time to set, then turn out on a platter and cut in squares to serve.

To make Birds in a Nest, make a dough of flour, water and lard, and line a large pan. Take a number of whole game birds and layer them with thick slices of bacon until the crust be filled. Scatter currants among the birds and season lightly. Cover with more of the crust, slash it and bake till it be done. Pour a dram of cider within to serve.

While it appears odd to bake whole birds within a pie, it seems the crust was used more as a serving vessel than as part of the actual dish. These can also be cooked in individual pie tins for ease of serving.

Birds in a Nest

2 lbs. small birds (or chicken thighs)
¼ lb. bacon
lard
currants
hard cider
½ tsp. salt
½ tsp. sage

pie crust

Prepare pie crust for a double crust pie and line a deep pie dish. Fill the crust with layers of chicken and bacon. Sprinkle the filling with currants and season with the salt and sage. Cover pie with second crust, crimping the edges to seal.

Slash crust in several places to vent and bake at 325°F for approximately one hour until the chicken is done and the crust is nicely browned.

To serve, pour a small amount of hard apple cider through the crust vents.

Large birds should be roasted and cut into pieces, and then cooked in a pot with good broth with egg yolks, and garlic and salt as well, and when the broth is thick it is done.

This recipe is one in a series of similar stews featuring roasted fowl. The ease of preparation and basic spicing make it an excellent representation of the type, and one which could easily be adapted to other varieties of poultry.

Stew of Roasted Chicken

2 lbs. chicken
2 cups broth
1 Tbsp. lard
1 cloves garlic
½ tsp. salt
2 egg yolks

Roast the chicken and then cut it into bite-sized pieces. Place the meat into a large pot with remaining ingredients and mix well. Cook over medium heat until it begins to boil and broth thickens. Serve hot.

Serves 6.

Warlord's Chicken - Take young fowl and grill them and chop until they be small. Mix eggs, anise, ginger and some salt with bread grated fine and mix with the fowl. Make the mixture to balls the size of a hen's egg, coat with bread crumbs and bake till they be full warm. Serve whole with Azagradag.

The original name of this recipe was simply "Warrior's Chicken". Margin notes state this was a dish much favored by the Warlord Khehrin Bladesmasher, and was renamed in his honor following his decisive victory in a battle with cave trolls. The notes also state that Khehrin lost several teeth in this battle, and the chicken's softer texture made it easier for him to eat.

Warlord's Chicken

1 lb. chicken, ground
2 eggs
½ tsp. ginger
¼ tsp. anise
½ tsp. salt
1 Tbsp. lard
½ cup bread crumbs

Mix ground chicken with the eggs, bread crumbs and spices. Make sure the mixture is not too wet, add more bread crumbs as needed. Roll the mixture into balls approximately 1½ inches in diameter, and roll in bread crumbs.

Bake at 325°F. If using pre-cooked chicken, bake until hot through. If starting with raw chicken, bake until internal temperature is 165°F.

Serve with a dish of the sour sauce for dipping.

Serves 4.

𝕬 stuffed and roasted young pig. 𝕿ake a small pig just a few weeks old and clean it well. 𝕿hen take the liver of the pig and eggs and bread and good herbs and some fat and mix them well, and place them into the pig and sew it closed. 𝕿hen roast the pig until it is done and serve it whole with a turnip in its mouth.

While a whole, stuffed piglet was a common "show dish" for Dwarven feasts, it is rather impractical for a modern household. We've reinterpreted the dish to be a stuffed pork loin, which retains the flavor and style of the original.

Stuffed Piglet

4 lbs. pork loin, whole
½ lb. pork liver
4 eggs
¼ lb. lard
½ lb. bread
2 Tbsp. parsley
2 Tbsp . herbs
½ tsp. salt

Cut bread and liver into 1 inch cubes and place in a large bowl. In a separate bowl, mix eggs, melted lard, bread, parsley, herbs, and salt. Pour over bread and liver and mix until bread and liver are just coated.

Slice pork loin open and fill with stuffing. Bake at 350°F until the meat reaches an internal temperature of 160°F.

Serves 12 to 16.

To make boar stew, get the flesh of a young pig and cut it in pieces, then take some shallots and chop them and cook them in fat, and put them with the pig in a pot. Add some good clean broth to the pot and some salt and good herbs, thyme and sage and celery seed that it have a good flavor, and boil it until it is done.

Below the original recipe is a note that this works best with a suckling pig, but any young pig will do. This is a basic, simply spiced stew, which would combine well with other dishes in a variety of menus.

Stew of Young Boar

2 lbs. pork
3 shallots
2 Tbsp. lard
2 cups broth
¼ tsp. salt
¼ tsp. thyme
¼ tsp. sage
¼ tsp. celery seed

Cut shallots into thin pieces and sauté in lard until tender. Cut up pork into half-inch pieces and place in a pot with onions and remaining ingredients. Bring to a boil, reduce heat, and simmer for one hour or until meat is tender.

Serves 6.

For a festive stew of boar, take the meat of a boar and grind it and cook it in oil with some onions. Add to this cinnamon and cloves and ginger and mace, along with some pepper and salt, and some vinegar. Put it all into a kettle with parsley and sage and a good amount of water and boil it, and serve it hot.

The notes appended to this recipe record that it was first brought to Kathaldûm by a traveling Halfling. The cook stated he was initially dubious about the range of spices included, especially when compared with the earlier, much simpler version. However, he also records that it was well-received and became a much favored dish.

Boar Stew

1 ½ lbs. ground pork
1 medium onion, chopped
2 Tbsp. olive oil
½ tsp. salt
¼ tsp. pepper
½ tsp. cinnamon
¼ tsp. cloves
¼ tsp. ginger
¼ tsp. mace
1 Tbsp. parsley
½ tsp. sage
2 cups water
¼ cup cider vinegar

Cook the onion with the oil in a large skillet until tender. Add ground pork and cook until the pork is no longer pink. Add remaining ingredients, bring to a boil, and then simmer for about 30 minutes.

Serves 6.

To make Khibed, make a dough from your stored breadstarter. Pull into balls the size of a hens egg and set aside. Boil the meat of a wild boar and chop it fine. Mix with chopped fatty bacon and tart apples. Season well with pepper. Fill each ball of dough with the meat and apples, taking care to seal the meat inside. Coat the dough with egg and bake till brown. Serve whole and do not damage.

There is some discussion that these meat rolls are a variant of Journeybread, though the filling would not keep as well as the nut and fruit version. The hearty bread dough would make the meat pies easier to transport than a short crust and would provide filling fare when there was no time for a formal meal.

Khibed

2 loaves frozen, unbaked bread dough, thawed (or 1
package frozen, unbaked rolls)
1 lb lean pork, boiled
¼ lb bacon
1 apple, chopped
1 egg
½ tsp pepper
½ cup grated light cheese (i.e. Gouda, Buttercheese,
Monterey Jack)

Thaw bread dough and let rise according to package
directions. If using loaves, cut each into 12 equal
pieces.

Boil the pork and chop fine. Combine with bacon
and apples, both chopped fine. Season with pepper
and a little salt, if desired. Add the grated cheese and
mix well.

Flatten each ball of dough. Divide meat and apple
mixture evenly among the pieces of dough. Seal the
mixture inside, pinching the dough and using the
egg beaten with a little water to seal. Place on a
baking sheet approximately 2" apart. Brush each
roll with the remaining egg wash. Bake until golden
brown.

To roast liver, take a good liver, cut in 5 pieces and roast the pieces then place in a pot with broth and cover it and cook it well. Let cool on a plate then take half of one piece and grind in a mortar with toasted bread till it be well mixed. Put then in a pot with spices, vinegar and honey and boil so it becomes thick. Add the liver pieces and serve.

A note scrawled in the margin states that this recipe had been tried with the livers of other game meats, but that it worked best with swine.

Roasted Pork Liver

1 lb. pork liver
2 cups broth
3 slices bread, toasted
1 tsp. ginger
½ tsp. anise
2 Tbsp. malt vinegar
1 Tbsp. honey

Cut the liver into large pieces and place in a stock pot with broth. Bring to a boil, reduce heat, and simmer until the liver is cooked - about 30 minutes.

Take about an ounce of the cooked liver and grind it with toasted bread in a mortar or food processor. Place it into a pot with anise, vinegar, honey, and the broth the liver was boiled in. Bring to a boil, reduce heat, and simmer until thick.

Place the remaining liver in a roasting pan, baste with sauce, and bake at 350°F until heated through. Serve hot with remaining sauce.

Serves 6.

Liver Zurid. Take the liver of a boar or pig and boil it and chop it well, then add eggs and bacon and raisins and salt. Then take caul fat and paint it with egg yolks, and put the liver on the fat and fold it over and tie it. Then place it in a pan and cook it, and cover it with more egg yolks colored green with parsley, and fry it well.

The use of caul fat to hold the filling suggests something rather sausage-like, but then the pieces are coated with green eggs and fried. The word *zurid*, which means something like "animal droppings", gives an indication of both the appearance of the final dish and the Dwarven sense of humor.

If caul fat is not available, thin sheets of fried eggs could be used in its place.

Chopped Liver Zurid

1 lb. pork liver
½ cup cooked bacon pieces
1 egg
¼ cup raisins
½ tsp. salt
caul fat

6 egg yolks
1 Tbsp. parsley, finely chopped
2 Tbsp. lard

Boil liver, allow to cool, and then chop or grind it
well. Add the bacon, egg, raisins, and salt and mix
well. Form the mixture into roughly two-ounce
portions, wrapping each portion in caul fat.

In a separate bowl, mix egg yolks and parsley well.
Dip the wrapped liver into the egg mixture and then
pan fry in lard until cooked.

Serves 6.

Take the intestines and stomach of a wild pig and boil them, then chop until they be small. Take parsley, sage and mint with eggs boiled hard and hearty caraway bread. Mix with pepper, a clear cider vinegar and good broth, taking care that it be not too sour. Pour over the boiled entrails, and add enough lard to make it rich. Let stand near the hearth until the stew become well warmed and thick. Season well and serve with more of the caraway bread.

While offal and many organ meats are 'specialty' foods to a modern palate, for cultures living off the land, no part of an animal could or would be wasted. Additionally, in leaner times, organ meats contain a higher fat content and thus would be more nutritionally dense.

Pork Tripe Stew

1 lb. pork chitterlings
1 Tbsp. parsley
1 tsp. mint
½ tsp. sage
4 eggs, boiled
3 slices bread
½ tsp. pepper
¼ cup vinegar (cider)
2 cups broth
1 tsp. salt

Boil the chitterlings in enough water to cover, and chop into small to medium pieces. Finely chop the herbs and combine with the coarsely chopped hard boiled eggs and bread which has been grated. Season with pepper. Combine the broth and vinegar in a stockpot, and add the herb and bread mixture. Stir in the chitterlings and let simmer over low heat until the stew begins to thicken. Season lightly with salt.

Serves 6.

To cook a boar's head, take it and put it to boil in equal parts water and wine, and when it is cooked remove the meat from the bones, removing the skin carefully that it be in one piece, and chop the meat and fry it with pepper and ginger, and lay out the skin all flat and spread the meat on the skin, and take apples that have been peeled and cored and nuts and raisins and chop them well together, and put them on the meat, and roll up the skin with all the rest inside, and then bake it until it is all hot.

Dwarves were in the habit of using as much of an animal as possible, and a boar's head would be highly prized for its meat and fat content. The addition of dried fruit, which would most likely have been imported, elevates the dish to a very high status, suitable for serving to nobility as a show piece in a major feast.

Boar's Head

1 boar or pig head
4 qts. water
4 qts. hard cider
1 tsp. pepper
½ tsp. ginger
2 apples
½ cup walnuts, chopped
1 cup raisins

Clean and singe the head and boil for 1 hour in water and cider. Remove from heat, drain, and allow to cool.

Cut the meat from the bone, carefully separating the skin from the meat. Chop the meat well and sauté it with the pepper and ginger.

Peel, core, and chop the apples. Mix with walnuts, raisins, and fried meat. Spread the skin out flat and cover with the mixture. Roll the skin up, tie it tightly, place in a roasting pan, and bake at 350°F to an internal temperature reaches 145°F.

Serves 8.

To make jelly, take the feet, ears, and tail of a pig or boar and clean them well, and put them into a kettle, and put some good wine and vinegar in the kettle as well, and add some salt and some pepper, and boil it all well until it is cooked, and skim it clean and strain it and put the liquid into a dish with some flesh and let it cool.

Unlike the gelatin typically served as a dessert, this is meant to be a savory dish, similar to many aspic recipes. Jelly was usually served in small bowls, and commonly included bits of meat or other choice morsels.

Pork Jelly

3 lbs. pig's feet
¼ lb. cooked pork, cut into small pieces
2 cups wine
¼ cup cider vinegar
1 ½ tsp. salt
¼ tsp. pepper

Place cleaned pigs feet in a large pot along with wine, vinegar, spices, and enough water to cover. Bring to a boil, reduce heat, and simmer until bones and meat are falling apart - about 4 hours. Strain liquid into a clean bowl over pork and allow to cool, skimming off the fat as necessary.

For roasted deer, let the meat lay overnight in ale, and then put it in a pot with some good broth, and add some onions and dark ale, and good spices, cover it well and let it cook in the great oven.

This recipe included margin notes in a later hand, recording observations on how it could be adapted for a variety of game. The second cook noted his adaptations for bear and wild goat - specifically recording the type of ale and mix of spices which worked best for each.

Roasted Venison

2 lbs. venison
2 cups ale (oatmeal stout)

1 cup broth
1 onion, chopped
½ tsp. ginger
¼ tsp. salt
½ tsp. pepper

Marinate the meat overnight in 1 cup of the ale.
Then place it in a dutch oven or casserole along with
remaining ingredients and bake at 350°F for 90
minutes or until internal temperature reaches 160°F.

Serves 6.

For Dîndâbathan, take a haunch of venison and roast on a spit, larding it well to keep the meat tender. To make the sauce, fry gân in fat and chop sweet apples and walnuts. Add together with cranberry mead, ginger, currants and pepper and let it all cook together. Pour over the venison and serve.

Dîndâbathan, roughly translated is "Hunter's Treat". The text states this was a favored autumn dish, when the deer were fattened for winter and both apples and walnuts were freshly gathered.

Gân are small rounds made of dark bread crumbs and honey, spiced with ginger and pepper. Frying them, then crumbling into the sauce would both serve as a thickener and add additional seasoning. A recipe for *gân* is given on page 96.

Venison in Sauce

2 lbs. venison
¼ lb. bacon
2 cups mead
6 gân, fried and crumbled
1 apple
¼ cup walnuts, coarsely chopped
½ tsp. ginger
½ tsp. pepper

Lay the venison in a roasting pan and cover with fatty bacon. Roast in a 325°F oven until the internal temperature is 160°F.

Fry the gân in lard (or butter if preferred). Combine cranberry mead and chopped apples in a pan with the spices. Crumble the fried gân into the sauce to thicken. Let simmer until flavors combine.

Ladle the sauce over the roast on a platter and serve.

Serves 6.

Take a haunch of red deer and cut to bits the size of a finger. Fry in a large kettle with lard and add thereto onions sliced thin and cook til they be tender. Add thyme, mustard, apple vinegar and sugar to the pot and season lightly with salt and pepper. Pour in a rich meat broth and a bit of hard cider to cover and bring to a boil and cook until it all be tender. Ladle over a thick slab of bread in a crock and so give out.

This stew would translate well to slow cooker preparation, though additional fat might be required for the longer cooking time.

Venison Stew

2 lbs. venison
2 onions, sliced
2 Tbsp. olive oil
¼ tsp. thyme
¼ tsp. mustard powder
1 Tbsp. cider vinegar
1 tsp. sugar
1 tsp. salt
½ tsp. pepper
1 cup meat broth
½ cup apple cider

Slice venison into thin strips and brown it in a large skillet with oil. Add onions and continue to cook until they are tender. Add remaining ingredients and bring to a boil. Reduce heat, cover, and cook for approximately 1 hour. Serve over bread or cooked root vegetables.

Serves 6.

Pigeon pie. Take pigeons and clean them, and chop parsley and sage and pepper and anise seed and salt, and put them on the pigeons, and wrap them in dough and bake them, and do not oversalt them.

The finished product of this recipe and the one which follows are similar to *Khibed*, in that they are meat filled pasties, though with more savory spicing. One could conclude the Dwarves favored these sort of filling, easily transportable tidbits as snacks – a way to 'fill in the corners' between more substantial meals.

If you wish, the chicken can be cooked before making the filling to reduce baking time.

Baked Pigeon Pies

1 lb. chicken
1 tsp. fresh parsley
1 tsp. fresh sage
½ tsp. salt
½ tsp. pepper
½ tsp. ginger
½ tsp. anise seed

pastry

Combine ground or chopped chicken with the spices and mix well.

Make a pastry dough with flour, water and lard and divide into twelve balls. Roll out each into a thin circle and place 1/12 of the filling onto one side. Fold the dough over the filling and crimp the edges to seal.

Bake at 325 until chicken is cooked and crust is golden brown.

Serves 4.

To make wrapped birds, take bread and hollow it out, and take small birds and boil them, and remove the meat from the bones, and chop it well, and add pine nuts and raisins, and put in some ginger and mix it well, and put it into the bread, and then take the bread and stop it up with dough, and wet the bread in a batter and fry it.

This recipe could be pan-fried, rather than deep fried. It could also adapt well to a beer batter.

If you prefer to make these like pasties, similar to the pies, simply replace the rolls with pastry crust.

Wrapped Birds

1 lb. chicken
6 rolls
¼ cup pine nuts
¼ cup raisins
½ tsp. ginger
½ tsp. cinnamon
¼ cup honey

batter for frying

Boil the chicken until it is cooked through, then cool and chop finely (or grind). Mix the cooked chicken with the pine nuts, raisins and ginger and set aside.

Cut a small hole in one side of each roll and hollow out, reserving the removed bread. Divide the filling evening among the rolls. Use the reserved bread, mixed with a little water, to fill the hole.

Mix a thin batter of flour, egg and water. Dip the rolls in the batter and deep fry.

Serves 4.

For a good soup of quail or other small birds, take some fennel roots and chop them, and boil them in good broth, and you can cook the livers of the birds with the fennel, and when it is done cooking, pour it over the birds that have been roasted with bacon.

While quail now have a reputation for being fancy food, for the Dwarves they were one of many small birds eaten when available. For a more economical variation, chicken thighs can be substituted and still retain the overall sense of the dish.

Quail and Fennel Soup

2 fennel roots
1 chicken liver (optional)
4 cups chicken broth
½ tsp. salt
½ tsp. ginger

6 boneless quail or chicken thighs
¼ lb. bacon

Cut fennel root into half inch cubes and place in a pot with broth and chicken liver and spices. Bring to a boil, and allow to simmer until fennel starts to soften - about 10 minutes.

Wrap the quail with bacon and broil until just cooked through, turning once halfway through - about 8 minutes total.

Place quail in separate bowls and top with broth and fennel pieces. Serve hot.

Serves 6.

For a boiled goose or other large bird, take it and put it in a pot of water with some salt, and see that it boils well. Then take milk and good new butter and some flour, and cook them all together with a little garlic and salt, and when it becomes thick then serve it with a young goose.

This dish is really two recipes in one. It has simple instructions for boiling a goose, and a sauce recipe that is very similar to a modern white sauce. One of the original authors noted that the sauce for this dish also goes well over mashed root vegetables.

Boiled Goose

1 goose, duck, or chicken

2 Tbsp. butter
2 Tbsp. flour
1 cup milk
2 cloves garlic, minced
¼ tsp. salt

Boil goose in a covered pot of salted water until tender.

Melt butter in a small saucepan. Whisk in flour until smooth. Then add milk and continue to whisk until thoroughly mixed. Add remaining ingredients, bring to a low boil, and simmer until thick.

Serves 6 - 8.

For a roasted goose, pluck it and clean it well, and put the liver to boil in water. Then take apples and peel them and remove the cores, and chop them and mix them with garlic and good herbs, and stuff this into the goose, and roast it well. Then take the liver and grind it to paste, and mix it with broth and vinegar, and spice it with anise and pepper and ginger, and put the sauce to boil and it should be thickened with bread crumbs.

Like the previous recipe, this one is made up of simple cooking instructions for the goose, and a more complicated sauce recipe.

In this case, the sauce makes use of cooked liver, and is similar to the sauce for the roasted pork liver recipe on page 26.

Roast Goose with Apples

1 goose
3 apples
1 Tbsp. parsley
1 tsp. sage
½ tsp. savory
1 clove garlic

1 goose liver
1 cup broth
1 egg, hard boiled
¼ cup cider vinegar
¼ tsp. anise seed
¼ tsp. pepper
¼ tsp. ginger
1 Tbsp. bread crumbs

Peel, core, and slice apples. Mix with parsley, sage, savory, and garlic, and stuff into goose. Roast goose to an internal temperature of 165°F.

Boil liver, allow to cool, and grind to a paste. Add remaining ingredients and mix well. Bring to a boil, simmer, and serve with roasted goose.

Serves 6 - 8.

For a boiled rabbit, take onions and fry them, and put them with cider and meat broth, and spice it with pepper, and set it to boil, and when it is boiled thicken it with bread and vinegar, and add a little ginger and salt before serving.

The combination of game meats and onions is very common in Dwarven recipes, as well as those from surrounding cultures. The acids in the onions help to tenderize the meat and to reduce the gamey flavor.

Rabbit in Sauce

2 lbs. rabbit
1 medium onion, chopped
2 Tbsp. lard
½ tsp. salt
½ tsp. pepper
¼ tsp. ginger
1 cup (2 slices) bread crumbs
½ cup hard cider
1 cup broth
2 Tbsp. cider vinegar

Sear pieces of meat briefly in a large pot and set aside, using lard as necessary. Cook onions in remaining lard until tender. Return the meat to the pot and add hard cider, broth, and pepper. Bring to a boil and simmer for one hour. Add bread crumbs, ginger, vinegar, and salt just before serving.

Serves 6.

For a stew of squirrels, clean and wash them well, and place them in a large baking dish with some water and vinegar and a little ginger. Then chop some onions and add them to the dish, and let it all rest undisturbed for some hours, and then remove the water and put it to cook with some more onions and carrots.

One of the cooks noted that this recipe was equally useful for other small game – marmots, weasels, field mice. Apparently, the acidity and spicing could be adjusted to make up for whatever the meat lacked.

Squirrel Stew

1 squirrel
½ cup vinegar
ginger
tarragon
2 onions, diced
2 carrots
water

Clean squirrel, washing thoroughly, and place it in a
large baking dish. Add vinegar, spices, and half of
the onions. Cover with water. Let stand for 2 to 3
hours, and then drain. Place in an oven at 350°F
until brown about 20 minutes. Add remaining onion,
carrots, cover, and cook until tender and broth
thickens.

Serves 4.

Sausage Recipes

As previously mentioned, the original text contained many sausage recipes. There were varying versions of several recipes in different parts of the texts – some differing little, others identical.

These sections of the text were among the most stained and dog-eared of the entire volume, suggesting heavy usage. It seems the idea of ground meats, stuffed into the animal's own intestines, appealed to the Dwarven sense of humor.

If you want to make good Zâr, take eight pounds of boar meat and chop it well. Then mix it with two pounds of bacon and chop it all together. Add to this some water, and some salt and pepper. Put in some sage and marjoram as well, and put it into clean sausage skins and it will be good Zâr.

The original text notes that every clan of dwarves had their own recipe for *Zâr* sausage. Most of the differences seem to center on the preferred spices and their proportions. In fact, this is one of the most duplicated recipes in the text. The final recipe below is representative of the minute variations. *Zâr* also seems to be the 'baseline' recipe from which the many other sausage variations derive.

Zâr Sausage

2 lbs. pork
½ lb. bacon
½ cup water
½ tsp. marjoram
½ tsp. sage
1 tsp. salt
3/4 tsp. pepper

sausage casing

Chop or grind the pork and bacon together. Mix with remaining ingredients and fill casing. Boil, bake, or fry sausage until its internal temperature reaches 160°F.

Serves 6.

For Zizâr, take boar or pork, and some pepper, and when it is chopped, put into it some bacon, diced. Make sure to take the bacon from the back and not the belly. When the sausages are firmly stuffed, hang them in the kitchen in the smoke and near the oven. This should be done before the moon is large, and if they are well and firmly filled then the Zizâr will remain good for a long time.

The text notes that this type of sausage was originally cold dried rather than being smoked. The cook recorded that during the great sickness, when large smoky fires were needed to fumigate the sick rooms, this was impossible, but the *Zizâr* made during that time was greatly improved both in flavor and longevity.

Zizâr - Smoked Sausage

2 lb. pork
½ lb bacon
1 tsp. salt
¼ tsp. pepper

sausage casing

Chop or grind pork and bacon. Mix well with remaining ingredients and fill casing. Place on a grill or smoker over indirect heat. Smoke at 250°F until the internal temperature reaches 160°F - about 1 hour.

Serves 8.

To make Khirzâr, take the tender meat of a boar or pig and half as much bacon and chop it all well. Then add grated cheese and salt and pepper and ginger and honey, and knead this all together. When it is well mixed, fill the sausage skins and tie them up at both ends. Then boil the Khirzâr for twice as long as it takes to cook an egg.

The combination of sharp cheese with the bite of ginger and the sweetness of honey made this sausage a favorite for breakfast. The notes stated that it was often served with spice cakes or oat porridge.

Khirzâr Sausage

1 lb. pork
½ lb. bacon
¼ lb. soft cheese
1 tsp. salt
1 ½ tsp. pepper
1 ½ tsp. ginger
1 tsp. honey

sausage casing

Chop or grind pork, bacon, and cheese. Mix well with remaining ingredients and fill casing. Boil, bake, or fry sausage until its internal temperature reaches 160°F.

Serves 6.

To make Zâr Nazîsh, take the liver and lungs from a deer, and the flesh as well as some pig fat and bacon, and chop it all well, and mix it with spices and then boil the sausage in a suitable broth.

While the original recipe calls for the lungs of the deer as well, we've left them out of this version as they are not commercially available. However, if you hunt and dress your own deer, feel free to include.

Zâr Nazîsh - Venison Sausage

1 lb. ground venison
½ lb. venison or pork liver
¼ cup lard
½ lb. bacon
½ tsp. ginger
1 tsp. pepper
1 tsp. salt

sausage casing
1 quart broth

Chop or grind venison, liver, lard, and bacon. Mix well with remaining ingredients and fill casing. Boil, bake, or fry sausage until its internal temperature reaches 160°F.

Serves 6.

To make Malugzâr, take partridges and pull the meat from the bones, then take the meat of a boar or pig and chop it all together well, and add some fat and some cumin and some chopped apples, then fill your zâr and it will be good.

If partridge is not available, this recipe could also be adapted for chicken, goose or duck. The spicing may need to be adjusted dependent on the gaminess of the fowl used.

Malugzâr - Sausage of Partridges

1 - 2 partridges
½ lb. pork
¼ cup lard
½ tsp. cumin
1 apple, chopped

sausage casing

Cut the partridge meat from the bone. Chop or grind it well, along with the pork. Mix with remaining ingredients and fill casing. Boil, bake, or fry sausage until its internal temperature reaches 160°F.

Serves 6.

To make good Urazârbanezn, first take the liver and lungs of a pig and chop them small, after that chop bacon into small pieces, and put salt and caraway seeds into it, but the liver and lungs must be cooked before they are chopped, and wet it all with as much of the broth as is enough, and then take the intestines and fill them, so that it will be good.

Given the number of liver recipes in the source, it's not surprising to find one among the sausage recipes. Here the liver was originally meant to be combined with lungs, however they can be difficult to find and are therefore omitted from the modern interpretation.

Urazârbanezn - Liver Sausage

2 lbs. pork liver, boiled
½ lb. bacon
1 tsp. salt
1 tsp. caraway
½ cup broth (approx.)

sausage casing

Chop or grind liver and bacon. Mix with remaining ingredients and fill casing. Boil or bake sausage until its internal temperature reaches 160°F.

Serves 6.

Khâthuzâr is made thus: take the stomach and intestines from small pigs and boil them, and add the fat from the kidneys, and cut it all together, then beat eggs and take a little bread and pepper and salt, and mix it all until the bread comes all apart, and put it with the intestines, and make the sausage with this and boil it well and give it out hot.

As with the preceding recipe for liver sausage, this recipe makes use of what most modern cooks would prefer to throw out. Here, the offal is mixed with bread to improve the texture.

Khâthuzâr - Pork Tripe Sausage

2 lbs. pork chitterlings
½ lb. lard
6 eggs
½ lb. bread
1 tsp. salt
½ tsp. pepper

sausage casing

Boil pork chitterlings, and grind them along with eggs and bread. Add remaining ingredients, mix well, and fill casing. Boil, bake, or fry sausage until its internal temperature reaches 160°F.

Serves 6.

For making Zârugnahzâr, take some good Khirzâr or Urazârbanezn or whatever kind of sausage pleases you, and grind it up, and put with it an equal amount of oats that have been well boiled, and some onion, and mix it all well, and spice it with salt and ginger, and then fill your zârugnahzâr and cook it like any other.

This recipe of sausage made from sausage appears to represent the somewhat wry sense of humor, either of Dwarves in general, or of this particular cook. It might also demonstrate a cultural frugality – using up whatever leftover bits were at hand.

Zârugnahzâr - "Sausage Sausage"

2 lbs. sausage
2 cups steel-cut oats, cooked
1 onion, chopped
2 tsp. salt
1 tsp. ginger

sausage casing

Grind sausage and mix well with remaining ingredients. Fill casing and boil, bake, or fry sausage until its internal temperature reaches 160°F.

Serves 8.

Umaralâm (Non-Meats)

From the text, *umaralâm* appears to mean "other" or "lesser". While the menus clearly show that Dwarves did eat non-animal foods, they were evidently not as prominent in the cuisine. It may also be that their diet was supplemented with other dishes, simple in preparation, such as boiled root vegetables, that the cooks did not deem necessary for inclusion in the text.

For a culture living primarily underground, eggs and dairy products would have been imported and therefore, luxury items. This may explain why tarts and custards using these ingredients are recorded in the text, while other vegetable dishes are not.

To make bread that is good for travel, take oats and cook them in water until they are done. Then mix them with honey that it be a little sweet and some salt and water just enough to make a thick paste. Then add some walnuts, chopped small, and mix it all well and put it into a large pan so it is not too thick, and bake it until it is dry. When it is a day old, cut it into pieces and wrap each piece in a clean cloth. If kept dry it will last many weeks.

Every culture has its own version of Journeybread. While that of the elves is generally held up as the standard, the Dwarven version is not without its devotees. The nuts provide basic protein, a staple of the Dwarven diet.

Dwarven Journeybread

½ cup butter, softened
½ cup honey
1 cup flour
¼ tsp. baking soda
¼ tsp. salt
1 ¼ cup rolled oats
½ cup finely chopped nuts
¼ cup currants (optional)

Combine butter and honey together and mix well. Add flour, baking soda, and salt, and mix until smooth. Stir in remaining ingredients and press into baking pan about ¼ inch deep. Bake at 350°F until done - about 25 minutes. Allow to cool for 10 minutes and then cut.

Serves 8.

For a rich pastry, take cheese and grate it and mix it with eggs and small pieces of fatty bacon. Then make a fine dough and fill it with the filling, and bake them in butter or fat, and serve them up when they are warm.

The cheese and eggs in these tarts make them more delicate and therefore less portable than the earlier pasties and stuffed bread. A mild white cheese – such as a Muenster or Monterey Jack – would blend well with the bacon and egg.

The original recipe calls for making these as closed pasties. With the raw egg, it is easier to make them in open tart shells baked in the oven. If you wish to adapt to closed pies, use chopped hard-cooked egg.

Rich Pastry

1 ½ cups cheese, grated or crumbled
2 eggs
½ cup cooked bacon pieces

dough
lard or butter

Add cheese and bacon to lightly beaten egg. Fill one large or several small pie crusts and bake at 325°F until crust is golden and egg is set.

Serves 2.

To make a pudding of carrots, take the carrots and boil them to make them soft, then grind them well and mix them with bread and eggs and honey, and spice it with coriander and a little salt. Then wrap this up in a fine cloth and boil it well, and then slice it and serve it sweet, and it is good with fruit and with mead.

This dish can be baked in a covered dish, cooked in a water bath, or steamed in a kettle. The result is a dense bread pudding that is not too sweet, and is excellent when flamed with brandy.

Carrot Pudding

½ lb. bread
4 carrots
1 cup milk
2 eggs
¼ cup honey
1 tsp. ground coriander
¼ tsp. salt

Boil carrots until tender, then drain and grind or chop finely. Add eggs, milk, honey, and spices and mix well. Cut bread into half-inch cubes, add them to the carrot mixture, and stir until the bread is well moistened. Put mixture into greased mold, ramekins, or casserole. Bake at 350°F for one hour. Serve hot, garnished with coarse sugar, fruit syrup, or brandy.

Serves 6.

To make a nut mash, grind the nuts in a mortar and put them into milk to soak, then add eggs and lard and honey and anise, and see that they're well mixed, and put this to bread cut into cubes. Cook it well and do not add too much salt.

The use of walnuts in this lightly sweetened bread pudding adds a slight bitterness that Dwarves appear to have favored. If desired, almonds or pecans could be used instead, and a little extra honey added to make it more appealing to the modern palate.

Nut Pudding

½ cup walnuts
1 cups milk
¼ lb. bread (about 5 slices)
2 Tbsp. honey
2 Tbsp. lard (or butter)
3 egg yolks
¼ tsp. salt
½ tsp. ground anise

Grind the walnuts finely and place in a large bowl with milk. Allow to rest for 20 minutes, stirring occasionally.

Cut the bread into small cubes, and place in a greased baking dish.

In a separate bowl, mix lard, egg yolks, honey, and spices. Combine with the nut and milk mixture, and then pour it all over the bread. Cover and bake in a 325°F oven for 45 minutes, or until a knife put into the center comes out clean.

Serves 6.

To make an apple tart, peel the apples and core them and grate them all small, and fry them in lard, then mix them with some cheese and some eggs, and spice it with ginger, and make it sweet with honey, and put it to bake in a crust.

Apples appear to have been one of the most common food items, both for the Dwarves as well as their neighbors. Similarly, the practice of making them into a sweet pie is also nearly universal.

Apple Tart

4 - 5 apples
2 Tbsp. lard

2 cups grated cheese
2 eggs
1 tsp. ginger
1 Tbsp. honey

short crust

Peel, core, and grate apples and fry in lard. Mix with remaining ingredients and put into pie shell. Bake at 350°F until done - about 50 minutes.

Serves 8.

For an egg tart, stir the eggs well with honey and a good amount of milk, and spice it with ginger. Make a crust of flour and fat in a pan, and put the filling into the crust and bake it well.

While this appears to be a simple dish, as noted earlier, the use of both eggs and milk would have made it a luxurious offering, meant for special occasions.

Egg Tart

6 eggs
4 cups milk
½ cups honey
½ tsp. ginger

pie crust

Mix eggs, honey, and ginger. Add milk, mixing well. Pour into tart shell and bake at 350°F for one hour, or until a knife inserted into the center comes out clean.

Serves 8.

To make fine cakes for a meal, take eggs and half as much milk, and the same amount of water, and add flour enough that it is a thin batter, and take fat and put it in a pan and heat it, and pour the batter into the pan and put it to bake, and when the batter is cooked, cut it in to strips and fry them gently in fat.

The batter should be thin in consistency, more for crepes than traditional pancakes. To serve, the cakes can be dusted with spices or served with honey and fruit.

Fine Cakes

2 eggs
½ cup milk
½ cup water
1 cup flour
lard

Mix eggs, milk and water, then add flour until it forms a thin batter. Grease a small skillet with the lard and cook thin cakes one at a time until they are well browned and dry. Transfer to a warmed platter until all the cakes are done.

Cut the cakes into long, narrow strips. Melt additional lard in a larger frying pan and stir fry the strips until they are crispy.

Serves 6.

For cabbage that will keep a long time, take the cabbage and chop it and mix it with some salt and caraway seeds. Then place it in a vessel and cover it with water and let it sit over the night. Then check it from time to time to make sure there is enough water, and take away any mold that forms, and so it should stay good for a month or more.

This dish would keep well through the winter, when stored in sealed crocks in a cool place. It would have provided nutritional variety when fresh produce was scarce.

Pickled Cabbage

5 lbs. cabbage
3 Tbsp. salt
2 tsp. caraway seeds
boiling water

Shred the cabbage and mix it well with the salt and spices. Pack the mixture into a large container along with boiling water enough to cover. Seal the container and store in the refrigerator overnight.

Serves 6.

For a strong cabbage with mustard, take the cabbage and cut it in pieces, and boil it until it is soft. Then take mustard and honey and caraway seeds, and mix them with some hard cider, and put the cabbage into this, and let it cool and serve it.

Another recipe for preserved cabbage. Here the stronger flavor of the mustard is well suited for game meats.

Strong Cabbage

1 head of cabbage
¼ cup stone-ground mustard
2 Tbsp. honey
2 Tbsp. hard cider
1 tsp. caraway seed

Cook cabbage in boiling water until just tender.
Drain and place in a large bowl with remaining
ingredients and mix well. Serve cold.

Serves 8.

To make a tart of green leaves, take the greens and pull them to pieces, and mix them with parsley and sage and marjoram, and chop them together, and add some eggs and grated bread, and sweeten it with honey, and then make a pastry shell and put all this in it and bake it as for a tart.

The amount of spicing and other ingredients almost makes it appear as though the cooks were trying to make the vegetables more palatable.

Greens can either be fresh or frozen, thawed and well drained.

Tart of Green Leaves

1 lb. chopped greens (spinach, chard, beet leaves, collards, cabbage)
1 Tbsp. parsley
1 tsp. marjoram
½ tsp. sage
½ cup parmesan cheese
4 eggs
1 cup (2 slices) bread crumbs
1 Tbsp. honey
sugar

pie crust

Mix all ingredients well and place in a pie shell. Bake at 350°F until done - about 50 minutes.

Serves 8.

Another way, take the greens and some old cheese, and a little lard, and some fresh cheese, and mix them all together, and make a good tart with this.

As with the previous recipe, this one does its best to add as much flavor as possible to the greens. In the margin near this recipe is a hastily scrawled note saying, "Trying to make food from what food eats."

A note scribbled in the margin by one of the later cooks stated that the flavor of the tart was much improved by the addition of chopped bacon and pine nuts.

Another Tart of Greens

1 lb. spinach or cabbage
1 cup chopped fresh herbs (sage, parsley, thyme, marjoram, watercress)
1 Tbsp. lard
½ cup parmesan cheese
¼ cup goat cheese
¼ teaspoon nutmeg
Salt and pepper to taste

pie crust

Blanch the greens briefly, chop them well, and place in a large bowl. Add remaining ingredients, mix well, and place in a pie crust. Cover with top crust and bake at 350°F until done - about 50 minutes.

Serves 8.

To make Gân, take honey and boil it, and skim it clean, and add ginger and pepper, and put in grated bread until it is thick enough to slice, and take this and make small cakes, and if they stick together then powder them with grated bread.

If serving with dessert, these honey cakes can be dusted with cinnamon or powdered sugar immediately prior to serving. Do not coat with sugar too soon, or the moist nature of the cakes will dissolve the sugar.

Gân - Honey Cakes

2 cups honey
2 pounds bread, grated
1 tsp. ginger (optional)
½ tsp. pepper (optional)

Bring honey to a boil, reduce heat, and simmer for about 15 minutes. Remove from heat, add spices, and mix in bread a cup at a time. Scoop out small portions and shape into a disk. Coat with bread crumbs if necessary, and allow to dry.

𝕿𝖔 𝖒𝖆𝖐𝖊 𝖆 𝖌𝖔𝖔𝖉 𝖉𝖎𝖘𝖍 𝖔𝖋 𝖔𝖆𝖙𝖘, 𝖇𝖔𝖎𝖑 𝖙𝖍𝖊 𝖔𝖆𝖙𝖘 𝖚𝖓𝖙𝖎𝖑 𝖙𝖍𝖊𝖞 𝖆𝖗𝖊 𝖆𝖑𝖑 𝖘𝖔𝖋𝖙, 𝖆𝖓𝖉 𝖕𝖚𝖙 𝖎𝖓 𝖊𝖌𝖌𝖘 𝖆𝖓𝖉 𝖒𝖎𝖝 𝖙𝖍𝖊𝖒, 𝖆𝖓𝖉 𝖎𝖋 𝖞𝖔𝖚 𝖜𝖎𝖘𝖍 𝖆𝖉𝖉 𝖘𝖕𝖎𝖈𝖊𝖘 𝖙𝖍𝖆𝖙 𝖎𝖙 𝖙𝖆𝖘𝖙𝖊 𝖜𝖊𝖑𝖑.

While oatmeal is now largely considered to be a breakfast food, the Dwarves often served it at dinner along side of roast pork or venison.

Oat Porridge

1 cup steel cut oats
3 ½ cups water
¼ tsp. salt
1 egg

½ tsp coriander or ginger (optional)

In a large pot, bring the water to a full boil. Add the oats and salt, reduce heat, and cook until soft - about 30 minutes.

Remove from heat, add egg and spices, and stir well.

Serves 4.

Note: If using quick-cooking oats, prepare them according to the instructions on the package.

To make a stew of apples, wash them clean and peel them and remove the core, and chop them all small, and put them with water enough and a little honey to make them sweet, and set them to boil until they are soft, and if it is too thin then add a little grated bread.

Apples were reasonably common in the woodland areas around Dwarven cities. Add to this the fact that apples would keep well in the cool air of caves and mines and it's no surprise that variations of this simple recipe appear in a number of Dwarven culinary manuscripts.

Stewed Apples

4 apples
3 cups water
¼ cup honey

grated bread (optional)

Peel, core, and chop apples, and place in a pot along with remaining ingredients. Bring to a boil and cook until apples are soft.

For a thicker dessert, add grated bread a little at a time as it cooks until it reaches the desired consistency.

Serves 6.

To make jellied mushrooms, take the tops of the mushrooms and fill them with eggs cooked hard all chopped up small, and add a little salt and good herbs, and the yolks of eggs, and when it is well cooked, pour jelly our broth over the mushrooms.

This dish falls somewhere between a stuffed mushroom appetizer and a soup. The rich jelly broth adds the fats that the mushrooms lack.

Jellied Mushrooms

8 mushrooms
3 eggs, hard boiled
1 egg yolk, raw
½ tsp. marjoram
¼ tsp. salt

1 cup meat jelly (p.33)

Clean mushrooms, removing and discarding the stem. Finely chop hard boiled eggs. Add egg yolk, marjoram, and salt and mix well. Put filling into mushroom caps and place them in a baking pan. Bake at 350°F for 40 minutes.

Heat jelly in a small saucepan until just melted. Pour over baked mushrooms before serving.

Serves 8.

Zozai (Sauces)

There are not many separate recipes for sauces in the text. It could be that these were not a staple of Dwarven cookery, and that spicing was the preferred method for flavoring. However, they are several sauces which are included in the main body of the recipe, rather than recorded in a different part of the text. (e.g., the Roast Goose with Apples on page 48)

To make azagradag, take sour apples and turnips and pound them together along with some parsley to make it green, and then cook it with a little salt.

This dish is more like a chutney or relish than what we might consider to be a sauce. Cooking reduces the strong flavor of the turnip, and the result is sweet, with a pleasant bite.

Azagradag - Sour Sauce

2 tart apples
1 turnip
2 Tbsp. parsley
½ tsp. salt

Finely chop or grind apples, turnip, and parsley.
Place in a saucepan with salt and enough water to
cover. Bring to a boil, reduce heat, and simmer for
15 to 20 minutes. Serve warm or cold.

Serves 6.

To make another sauce, take shallots and peel them and chop them small, and mix them with parsley, and wet it all with mead and vinegar, and this sauce is good to serve on boar or small birds.

This relish-like sauce gets balances the tartness from the vinegar with sweetness from the combination of onion and mead.

Sauce for Boar or Game Birds

1 cup shallots, finely chopped
1 Tbsp. parsley
½ tsp. salt
2 Tbsp. mead
2 Tbsp. malt vinegar

Mix all ingredients together and refrigerate
overnight to allow flavors to mingle.

Serves 6.

To make pepper sauce, take bread and brown it over the fire until it starts to blacken on both sides, then put it with broth, and strain it, and mix the broth with onions that have been chopped well and some bacon, and cook it well, and then add some vinegar, and it will taste like pepper sauce.

There is a certain irony in the chef labeling this as simply 'pepper sauce' when it contains no pepper. The bite of the sauce comes from the blackened bread and vinegar.

Pepper Sauce

3 slices bread
1 cup broth
¼ cup cider vinegar
1 onion, chopped
¼ cup chopped bacon

Toast bread until it starts to burn, and then tear up into small pieces. Add broth and vinegar, allow to soak for 15 minutes, and then strain into a saucepan, discarding the solids. Add remaining ingredients, bring to a boil, reduce heat and simmer until onions are tender. Serve hot.

Serves 6.

Khazn (Things to Drink)

The text contains surprisingly few beverage recipes, especially given how many varieties are used in the recipes and the quantities which are noted in the menus.

It may have been that the cooks who recorded this text were not brewers themselves, and therefore only recorded directions for the out of the ordinary vintages. There may also have been a separate brewer's guide, containing the instructions for day to day brews, which is now lost.

To make a good mead, take water and honey, allowing four gallons of water for each gallon of honey, and add the whites of an egg for each gallon, and put this into a kettle along with a handful or two of oak leaves and boil it, and take away the froth that comes to the top, and when it is done set it to cool. When it is all cool put in a little yeast, and cover it and let the yeast thrive, and when that is done put it into bottles and do not drink it for many weeks.

The original source for this recipe calls for oak leaves, presumably for the tannins, however that would add a potentially unpleasant flavor. The recipe below uses commercial grape tannin, but 1 cup of very strong tea may be used instead.

Basic Mead

1 qt. (3 lbs.) honey
1 gallon water
1 egg white
1/8 tsp. grape tannin
1 pkg. (2 tsp.) wine yeast

Place honey, water, and the egg white in a large
kettle and bring to a boil, reduce heat, and simmer,
stirring continuously. Skim off and discard any
scum that forms on the surface. Continue simmering
until there is no more scum to remove. Add tannin
and remove from heat. Cover and allow to cool
overnight. Add yeast and transfer to a fermenting
bottle with a vapor lock. Rack (to remove
sediments) when fermentation stops, and again three
months later. Bottle when the mead is clear, and
store in a cool, dark place for a couple of months
before drinking.

For a savory mead, take water and honey as descibed before and put this into a kettle along with greens and fennel that have been chopped, and then boil it well, and when it is done and any froth has been removed, set it to cool and then put in a quarter pint of new yeast, and cover it well and tight. When the fermenting is done put it into bottles and let it age right.

To the modern palate, the idea of a 'savory' mead seems somewhat unlikely. However, the balance of sweetness from the honey and tart, earthy greens can provide an interesting dimension to the often strong flavors of game meats. It is also another way of including vegetables in the diet without actually eating them.

Savory Mead

1 qt. (3 lbs.) honey
1 gallon water
½ lb. spinach, chopped
1 fennel root, chopped
1 pkg. (2 tsp.) wine yeast

Place honey, water, spinach and fennel into a large kettle and bring to a boil, reduce heat, and simmer, stirring continuously. Skim off and discard any scum that forms on the surface. Continue simmering until there is no more scum to remove. Remove from heat, cover, and allow to cool overnight. Add yeast and transfer to a fermenting bottle with a vapor lock. Rack (to remove sediments) when fermentation stops, and again three months later. Bottle when the mead is clear, and store in a cool, dark place for a couple of months before drinking.

For a drink of parsnips, take the roots and boil them, and then mash them and put them in a kettle, and then add to the parsnips some water and the juice of sloes and a little honey. Set this all to boil a while and then let it all to cool, and then add some good yeast and set it to ferment. It will be an odd color, but will taste well.

The addition of sloe juice gives a strange color to an already strange drink. One can only imagine that when given an abundance of root vegetables, Dwarven brewers tried to find as many ways as possible to use them.

Parsnip Wine

4 lbs. parsnips
1 gallon water
1 pint sloe juice
1 pint honey
1 pkg. (2 tsp.) wine yeast

Boil parsnips in water until soft. Drain them and mash well. Place the mash into a kettle along with the water, sloe juice, and honey. Bring to a boil, reduce heat, and simmer, stirring continuously, for 30 minutes. Remove from heat, cover, and allow to cool overnight. Add yeast and transfer to a fermenting vessel covered by a cloth towel. After 5 days, transfer to a fermenting bottle with a vapor lock, leaving behind any pulp and sediments. Rack when fermentation stops, and again three months later. Bottle when the wine is clear, and store in a cool, dark place.

For a strong ale, take turnips and roast them until they are soft, and chop them small, and boil water enough for the ale, and put in the turnips along with the grain, and boil it and then let it cool, and when it is cool put in the yeast, and cover your butt head with a sheet, and set it to ferment.

It may be this was an invention born of necessity for which the residents of Kathaldûm developed a taste. After all, anything with a natural sugar content can be encouraged to ferment.

Turnip Stout

10 lbs. malted grain
5 lbs. turnips, roasted and chopped
10 gallons water
10 grams ale yeast
¾ cups honey

Heat 3 gallons of water to 155°F. Add grain and turnips, stir, and allow to rest at that temperature for an hour. Carefully bring the temperature up to 170°F, stirring the mash continuously. *Do not let it get above 172°F.* Hold this temperature for five minutes.

In a separate kettle, heat remaining water to 170°F and add to mash. Strain, repeating as necessary until liquid no longer has chunks of mash. Bring the liquid - called *wort* - to a boil. Keep it boiling for 1 hour, stirring regularly.

Cover and allow wort to cool to 75°F. Rack the wort into the primary fermenter and add the yeast. After a week of fermentation, rack and allow to ferment an additional two weeks. Rack again and bottle, priming with ¾ cup of honey.

Nagindalu (Menus)

This section appears to be more a record of what had
been done than directions on how to plan a
particular kind of celebration. Scribbled in the last
few pages in the lattermost hand, it is almost as
though the last cook was recording notes, legends,
and descriptions of feasts through the ages so he
would know what to do should he be required to
stage a similar event. Margin notes make it seem as
if the recorder does not believe the feasts occurred
quite the way they were remembered.

Menu for the Coronation of Thorfil Axewielder On His Taking the Throne at the Great City of Kathaldûm

First Course: Dry Sausage, Roasted Pork, Roasted Goose, Cooked Greens.

Amusement: A boar's head, roasted and painted in the colors of the new King.

Second Course: Venison Stew, Roasted Heron, Jellied Mice and Squirrels, Cooked Roots.

Amusement: An army of small, roasted birds, each with an axe and shield and helm, attacking a fortress.

Third Course: Small Sausages, Fine Cakes, Mead.

Amusement: A great carrot pudding, covered in spirits and set aflame.

Menu for the Wedding of Enaig, Daughter of Eunror Stonecutter, and Brunnur, heir to the Axe of Molordûn

First Course: Khirzâr sausage and mustard, Roasted Geese, a dish of a hundred birds, Turnips in Broth.

Second Course: Oat cakes and Pork Tripe Sausages, strong cabbage and stronger mead.

A piglet, split open along its spine and turned inside-out, and stuffed with piglet's liver, well beaten with good spices, and cheese and eggs and fruits, and then roasted.

Third Course: Sausages of partridges, sour sauce, egg tarts, honey glazed sausages.

Several dozen little sausages to throw at the bride.

Provisions for the Funeral of the Bardur, who was the son of Durgonir and cousin to the King

For one hundred and twenty mourners, the following items were needed.

Four wild boars.
Thirty ducks, geese, and wild hens.
Two hundred small birds.
One hundred and ten eggs.
Eighty pounds of smoked sausages.
Many plants for sundry recipes.
One hundred and forty gallons of small ale.
Fifty gallons of mead.
Ten gallons of distilled mead.
One cask of very fine blackberry wine to accompany the departed.

www.ingramcontent.com/pod-product-compliance
Lightning Source LLC
Chambersburg PA
CBHW071004040426
42443CB00007B/655